MARK E. KENNICOTT

WHERE

VIRTUE

FLOWS

Receiving the Power
Released in His Presence

WESTBOW
PRESS®
A DIVISION OF THOMAS NELSON
& ZONDERVAN

Scripture taken from the New King James Version®. Copyright © 1982 by Thomas Nelson. Used by permission. All rights reserved.

Scripture quotations marked (NIV) are taken from the Holy Bible, New International Version®, NIV®. Copyright © 1973, 1978, 1984, 2011 by Biblica, Inc.™ Used by permission of Zondervan. All rights reserved worldwide. www.zondervan.com The "NIV" and "New International Version" are trademarks registered in the United States Patent and Trademark Office by Biblica, Inc

Scripture quotations marked (NLT) are taken from the Holy Bible, New Living Translation, copyright ©1996, 2004, 2007, 2013, 2015 by Tyndale House Foundation. Used by permission of Tyndale House Publishers, Inc., Carol Stream, Illinois 60188. All rights reserved.

Scripture quotations marked MSG are taken from THE MESSAGE, copyright © 1993, 1994, 1995, 1996, 2000, 2001, 2002 by Eugene H. Peterson. Used by permission of NavPress. All rights reserved. Represented by Tyndale House Publishers, Inc.

WestBow Press books may be ordered through booksellers or by contacting:

WestBow Press
A Division of Thomas Nelson & Zondervan
1663 Liberty Drive
Bloomington, IN 47403
www.westbowpress.com
1 (866) 928-1240

ISBN: 978-1-9736-1856-0 (sc)
ISBN: 978-1-9736-1857-7 (hc)
ISBN: 978-1-9736-1858-4 (e)

Library of Congress Control Number: 2018901622

Print information available on the last page.

WestBow Press rev. date: 03/01/2018

For Zulmita, my wife and best friend; for Zachary, Joshua, Elena, and Elisa, my children and my world; and for Jesus Christ, the One who baptizes with the Holy Spirit and with fire.

CONTENTS

PREFACE

We take our eyes for granted. When we roll out of bed in the morning and take a casual look around the room, we seldom (if ever) think about the work our eyes are doing to make sense of the world. When we look out the window to take in the first rays of daylight, we might gasp in delight over the beauty of the morning sky, but we attribute that beauty to the color of the sky itself. We certainly are not awestruck by the capacity of our brains to decipher the intricate details captured by the rods and cones of the eyes, the tiny internal receptors that make it possible to distinguish *millions* of colors. We just see. But if those internal processes faltered, the separation of light necessary to see certain colors would fail, leading to varied types of color-blindness. We could look at the same sunrise and see an entirely different vista.

It turns out that nearly three hundred million people worldwide are affected by red-green colorblindness and see the world around them quite differently than the rest of us. Where we might see vibrant color, they see dingy gray. In 2010, a team of scientists set out to develop a solution to the problem, and within just two years they were able to produce glasses to help people see full color for the very first time.

The results have been beautiful and inspiring.

Videos of people putting on the glasses for the first time have been popular on social media (visit enchroma. com). Whether children or grown adults, the first reaction is consistently similar: tears, then laughter, and then more tears. They can't believe the world looks so beautiful. It is a remarkable and heartwarming thing to behold.

I have had a similar experience with the Scriptures. Living two thousand years after the fact, removed by culture, time, language, and distance, I couldn't help but read the Bible with very different eyes than did its original Middle Eastern and Mediterranean audience. My internal wiring only allowed me to perceive certain hues of the Scripture's internal beauty. It was enough to come to saving faith in Christ, which is the most important thing, but my understanding of the Scriptures at times felt two-dimensional, black and white, lackluster. There was more there; *I just couldn't see it.*

Then in 1992, a minister in our church returned from an out-of-state conference with a cassette-tape teaching series that changed my world. It was a twelve-lesson series titled *Our Hebrew Lord*, taught by Dwight A. Pryor (of blessed memory), the president of The Center for Judaic-Christian Studies (visit jcstudies.org). In a series of lectures, Dwight took me back to the Jewish world in which Jesus lived and removed layers of cultural, linguistic, and historical soot that had collected on the lenses through which I read the Scriptures. He gave me new glasses to look through as I beheld the life and teaching of Jesus, and it was suddenly alive with new color!

It was like that moment in *The Wizard of Oz*, when Dorothy finds herself over the rainbow and steps out of her house for the first time in the Land of Oz. The movie, which had begun in black and white, suddenly burst forth into vibrant Technicolor. That is the way the Bible seemed to me. It was a whole new world.

In the years since, studying the cultural, linguistic, and historical context of Jesus's life, ministry, and teachings has been a personal passion, spilling over into my own ministry of teaching, pastoring, and now writing. I want to dedicate this book in part to Dwight's memory, as he was used by God at a very formative time in my life.

My prayer is that what you read in the pages ahead will have a similar effect on you that Dwight's teaching had on me. Not that I esteem myself to be any great shakes as a teacher or writer, but rather because I hope to bring out of the Scriptures some wonderful colors that you might not have seen before. I invite you to look at the Bible with new eyes and allow the beauty of God's story to leave you awestruck at His majesty. If this book can accomplish that, I will consider my efforts a success.

—Mark E. Kennicott, March 12, 2017

INTRODUCTION

Jesus had a way of meeting people in the margins, of touching the untouchable and loving the unlovable. Perhaps that is why so many New Testament stories resonate deeply with us, even with the distance of time, language, and culture, which separates us. A Canaanite woman with a tortured daughter. A tax collector despised by his countrymen. A man born blind, begging by the roadside. A leper forced to live outside the city. A woman with an issue of blood. We read their stories today,[1] and even two thousand years removed, it feels personal. We can identify with them being on the outside because that is how we feel. We feel their pain because it is our pain; we identify with their struggles because they are our struggles. *Their stories are our stories.* And because each of them had a life-changing encounter with Jesus, we somehow feel hope for our own circumstances. If Jesus could meet them, *He can meet us.* If Jesus could change them, *He can change us.*

Perhaps that is why the Holy Spirit inspired the Gospel writers to include these stories in the sacred story we call the Bible; not merely to document the miraculous deeds of Jesus's ministry, but to hold out hope for the rest of us. To allow each story to serve as a visual aid to God's continuing desire to save, to deliver, and to heal. To paint a path forward for those who find themselves in similar circumstances but don't know how to take the next step. The lessons we learn from these encounters can teach us about our Savior, even as they teach us about ourselves, and provide us with valuable insights on how we might approach Jesus in our own times.

That lesson is perhaps most striking in the story of the woman with the issue of blood, which is the subject of this book. The bulk of this treatment can be traced to a sermon that I have preached on several occasions, usually by the same title, or some variation of it. Through careful study and prayerful reflection, I have concluded that there are at least three elements to this unnamed woman's story that are deeply significant for us today: her desperate need, her determined heart, and her daring faith. Drawing these themes out of the text will be the main effort of this short book, with a concluding chapter to make an important personal application.

Let's take a moment to survey her story:[2]

Now a certain woman had a flow of blood for twelve years, and had suffered many things from many physicians. She had spent all that she had and was no better, but rather grew worse. When she heard about Jesus, she came behind Him in the crowd and touched His garment. For she said, "If only I may touch His clothes, I shall be made well." Immediately the fountain of her blood was dried up, and she felt in her body that she was healed of the affliction. And Jesus, immediately knowing in Himself that power had gone out of Him, turned around in the crowd and said, "Who touched My clothes?" But His disciples said to Him, "You see the multitude thronging You, and You say, 'Who touched Me?' And He looked around to see her who had done this thing. But the woman, fearing and trembling, knowing what had happened to her, came and fell down before Him and told Him the whole truth. And He said to her, "Daughter, your faith has made you well. Go in peace, and be healed of your affliction."

She had what the King James Version of the Bible calls "an issue of blood," an incurable hemorrhage that only got worse with time, even though she paid for the best medical treatment available (Luke 8:43). Then one day, she heard about a man from Galilee who was doing the miraculous. Blind eyes were being opened! The lame were walking! The deaf were hearing! Something within her own heart leapt with hope. *I don't have to stay this way. I can be healed!*

With unshakable resolve, she found her way to where Jesus was. She spied Him through the crowd and thought, *If I can just touch His clothes, I will be healed!* She forced her way through the swarming entourage, finally inching her way on hands and knees until her prize was within reach. Then, in a moment of truth, she reached out and laid hold of her miracle.

I'll save the rest for later. Suffice it to say, her story made such an impact on those around Jesus that day that three out of four Gospel writers included it in their narratives, and we are still talking about her today.

That being the case, one wonders what could possibly be said that we have not already heard. After all, adding all three Gospel accounts together, this incident comprises a grand total of only nineteen verses. Is that enough to merit the writing (or the reading) of an entire book, even a small one like this?

Absolutely.

I intend on taking you on a journey that will not only flesh out the details of this beautiful story, but will also reveal how her story is really *your story*, and how the lessons learned from this ancient text can make a difference in your life today.

You see, in the very moment she laid hold of Jesus, something extraordinary happened. Something happened for her that will just as certainly happen for you. *Virtue flowed into her.* The word *virtue* is King James

English for *power*. In Chapter Four we will explore its meaning in more depth, but for now, let's just consider what it meant for this woman: healing, wholeness, and restoration. She would never be the same again.

Let me make you a promise. If you will open your heart and receive with faith the message contained in this little book, *you too will never be the same*. Like her, you will find yourself in the most unlikely yet the most rewarding place, the place in His presence *where virtue flows*.

Chapter One

A Desperate Need

Only when we understand our depravity can we appreciate His
sufficiency.

We don't know her name, but three out of four
Gospel writers tell us her story. In Mark 5:25 she is called
a "certain woman, who had a flow of blood for twelve
years." Not only was she subject to bleeding, but the
Scripture adds that she "had suffered many things from
many physicians. She had spent all that she had and was
no better, but rather grew worse" (v. 26). This assessment
of her condition from the Gospel narrative seems so

straightforward and matter-of-fact that we might easily miss many important implications. But looking closer, this seemingly nonchalant appraisal speaks volumes about her social status and her state of mind. And as we will see together, it also speaks volumes about us.

First, the Bible tells us that she had a "flow of blood" that apparently had not gone away *for twelve years.* That is significant, because in Leviticus 15:25 we find that she would have been considered "unclean," a condition that would have forced her from her home and placed her outside the city (perhaps to live in a leper colony) until her flow of blood was healed. Over the course of twelve years, her life would have dramatically changed, as the social stigma and civil regulations related to her condition effectively made her a social outcast. Friends and family would be a thing of the past; in fact, we might even surmise that she had no one left to care for her at all. Either she had never married (what man would want to enter a marriage that he could not consummate?), she had been "put away" in divorce (presuming her condition began while she was married), or she was widowed. Whatever the case, she was likely all alone; her condition had ruined her life.

Second, the fact that she had "spent all she had" on medical care suggests that at one time she had had significant (though perhaps not extravagant) wealth, as it is unlikely that the Gospel writers would have included such information if she had little to spend on doctors to begin with. While we can only guess where her money came from, we can see clearly where it went. Not only did she spend it on many doctors, but the text tells us that she "suffered many things" at their hands. This suffering was likely due to the primitive and superstitious practices of the medical care of her day.[3] Some of the remedies for people in her condition during that time included drinking various concoctions of wine, onions, cumin, crocus, and fenugreek (a pungent aromatic seed), as well as unusual scare tactics that were more likely to cure the hiccups than a case of bleeding. Unlike the care we receive today, which generally preserves the dignity of the patient (except for those awful open-back gowns!), this woman endured much humiliation and abuse, only adding to her suffering.

She was destitute, she was desperate, and she had lost all hope. She could not interact meaningfully with others, and she was constantly being reminded of her condition with each shout of "Unclean!" that she was forced to yell as she warned others to keep their distance. She had truly come to the end of herself, and that is why she is so instructive for us; *that is exactly how we need to see ourselves.*

The reason that we don't often see God work in our own lives is because we don't fully realize *how badly we need Him.* We need to become like this woman: spiritually destitute, desperate for change, and devoid of any hope or trust in ourselves. Only then can we find ourselves in a position where virtue can flow.

When All Else Fails

What does it take for someone to become truly desperate for God? What is the boiling point in our lives when we finally turn to Heaven for answers? For most of us, the answer is simple enough. We turn to God *when all else fails,* or said another way, when we come to the end of our rope. We look to God for answers only when we can't answer life's problems on our own. In short, *God is our last resort.* We only want God to manage the unmanageable, and we'll handle everything else, thank you very much.

Self-reliance is the celebrated hallmark of the

human spirit, especially in the West. It seems that we are taught from childhood to rely on own strength, our own talent, our own intellect, and our own resources, turning to God for help only when they fail to be enough. "If it ain't broke," we say, "don't fix it." Don't ask for help, don't admit when you're wrong, and—especially if you're a man—*never* stop and ask for directions. We seem to come prewired with an attitude of self-sufficiency. Even after we become Christ followers, we fall prey to this mentality. We may grow to trust God in times of weakness, but we really don't see the need to lean on Him when we feel strong, when we think we've got it all together. But the truth is that without Jesus, we really don't have it all together. And unfortunately, we don't usually recognize that truth until tragedy strikes.

Jesus spoke to the heart of this reality when He said, "Those who are well have no need of a physician, but those who are sick" (Mark 2:17). This seems like a rather obvious statement until you examine the context. Let's take a closer look.

As an itinerant rabbi and teacher, Jesus was often invited to the homes of religious leaders, such as the teachers of the Law and the Pharisees. In most cases, they simply wanted to test Jesus (or more precisely, to *trick* Jesus) into saying or doing something that they could later use against Him. In this case, Jesus actually invited Himself to dinner. With whom did Jesus seek to dine? Perhaps a popular politician? A well-connected priest? A venerable rabbi, or a dignified Pharisee?

None of these.

Jesus invited Himself to eat with a socially despised tax collector. The nerve! The chutzpa! No dignified Jew would grace the home of such a sinner, let alone eat with him. But this wouldn't be the first time that Jesus would offend the delicate sensitivities of the dignified! While the religious elite of His day were chattering in disbelief, the Scripture says that even more sinners and tax collectors gathered in and sat down with Jesus. Evidently, the spectacle became too much for some of them to bear, for someone finally spoke up. To His disciples they demanded, "How *is it* that He eats and drinks with tax collectors and sinners?" (Mark 2:16). It was to this condemning inquisition that Jesus replied, "Those who are well have no need of a physician, but those who are sick." He then added, "I did not come to call *the* righteous, but sinners, to repentance" (v. 17).

Now hold on just a second! Were the scribes and Pharisees *truly* righteous? Did Jesus really intend to give them that kind of credit? It seems unlikely given the fact that Jesus minced no words denouncing the hypocrisy of the supercilious. He called them "blind guides" and "a brood of vipers," among other things. For a full picture of how Jesus felt about many of the religious leaders of His day, read Matthew 23. Here's a snapshot from verse 15:

> Woe to you, scribes and Pharisees, hypocrites! For you travel land and sea to win one proselyte, and when he is won, you make him twice as much a son of hell as yourselves.

Ouch! Obviously, Jesus was not suggesting that these so-called righteous were actually righteous! These "well" people were anything but well, but that is exactly the truth that Jesus was driving at. *Those who do not believe they are sick do not solicit the help of a physician.* People who "have it all together" don't *need* God. Or said more accurately, those *who think* they have it all together don't *see* their need for God. Instead, they look at those who confess their need with disdain, as did one politician who said in recent years, "Religion is for weak people with weak minds." To them, faith is just a crutch.

But that is the point, isn't it? Only those who are crippled see their need for crutches. However, the Gospel does so much more than prop us up. *Jesus gives us new legs.* The truth is that we are *all* cripples apart from Christ. Without Jesus, we truly don't have a leg to stand on. All our goodness, all our benevolence, and all our righteousness counts for nothing—*less than nothing*—compared to the absolute standard of God's holiness. None of us can stand before God based on our own merits. We are lost, undone, unrighteous, and unholy.

The difficulty is getting people to recognize their condition. We are like the ones James describes, who look at ourselves in the mirror and then walk away, forgetting what we saw (James 1:23).

Have Mercy On Me!

The Pharisees were not willing to admit that they needed the grace of God. They were so comfortable with their religious performance that they did not recognize their utter spiritual bankruptcy. Jesus exposed their crippling self-righteousness one day in the following parable:

> Two men went up to the temple to pray, one a Pharisee and the other a tax collector. The Pharisee stood and prayed thus with himself, "God, I thank You that I am not like other men—extortioners, unjust, adulterers, or even as this tax collector. I fast twice a week; I give tithes of all that I possess." And the tax collector, standing afar off, would not so much as raise *his* eyes to heaven, but beat his breast, saying, *"God, be merciful to me a sinner!"* I tell you, this man went down to his house justified *rather* than the other; for everyone who exalts himself will be humbled, and he who humbles himself will be exalted. (Luke 18:9–14, emphasis added).

In this dramatic parable, Jesus criticizes the Pharisees for their sense of self-righteousness by contrasting them with the most despised member of their society, the tax collector. The tax collector was the man that everyone loved to hate, the political turncoat despised by his countrymen for being in collusion with the Romans. And yet, Jesus turns the conventional perception on its head, suggesting that this man, rather than the self-righteous Pharisee, is the kind of man that God takes notice of. The tax collector, not the Pharisee, is the man that we all need to be like, *a man who knows he needs God,* a man who has no confidence in his own performance, a man who knows beyond the shadow of a doubt that only God can justify. And justify He does, when our hearts cry out like this poor soul, "Have mercy on me a sinner!"

Calling him a "poor soul" is quite accurate, by the way. He recognized his own complete and utter spiritual bankruptcy. This is what the Bible calls being "poor in spirit." Jesus said, "Blessed are the poor in spirit, for theirs is the kingdom of Heaven" (Matthew 5:3). No wonder this man went home justified! He knew through humility something the Pharisee could not perceive through his pride: *where he stood with God.* He understood his own depravity; therefore, he could appreciate God's sufficiency.

How about you? You may feel like you have more in common with the Pharisee in Jesus's parable. You pray and fast, you read your Bible every day or at least most days. You don't engage in any gross sins, maybe just a few refined and well-hidden ones. You attend church faithfully, and overall you feel confident that you are a good person. If that's you, let me remind you:

> There is no one righteous, not even one; there is no one who understands, no one who seeks God. All have turned away, they have together become worthless; there is no one who does good, not even one. (Romans 3:10–12)

The truth is, no matter how good we are or how glowing our spiritual résumé,[4] we are all in desperate need of the justification that only God can give. Knowing how far God had to reach down to lift us up offers fresh perspective to our faith; it helps us remember that grace is by definition *unmerited*. We all need Him, and the Bible says we are blessed when we know it. Let's look again at Matthew 5:3, only this time in the New Living Translation (NLT):

> God blesses those who realize their need for Him, for the Kingdom of Heaven is given to them.

Did you get that? God blesses those *who realize how much they need Him.* God eagerly waits to give us "the kingdom of Heaven" (the expression of His ruling authority and influence) when we concede how desperate for Him we really are. No wonder The Message paraphrase of this verse reads, "You're blessed when you're at the end of your rope. With less of you there is more of God and his rule." Amen! Only when you come to the end of yourself can you discover the beginning of Him.

The woman in our story had come to the end of her rope. She knew her condition was desperate, and she knew that there was nothing she could do to change it by her own wisdom, intellect, or resources. That's one reason why we can so easily identify with her story. We've all been in that same place of desperation. We've all felt the hopelessness of helplessness, and we've all wondered if things would ever change.

Pressing Through Today

Desperation is a tricky subject for many Christians because while they might affirm its priority in their conversion, they do not see it as an important element of their ongoing life of faith. To be clear, I am not advocating a sense of spiritual insecurity that causes us to constantly question our salvation or second guess our status as children of God. No, what I am advocating is a holy discontentment that groans for more of God and an absolute dependence on Jesus in the everyday stuff of life, recognizing that the grace that saves us is the grace that keeps us. The moment we misplace our confidence by trusting in our own goodness, holiness, or accomplishment is the moment we sabotage the foundations of our faith. The moment we think that we're doing God a favor by being at church, or doing His work, or whatever, is when we've forgotten the clear teaching of Jesus when He said, "Without me you can do nothing" (John 15:5b). Regardless of the length or depth of our walk with God, the cry of our hearts must remain,

> *I need thee, O I need thee!*
> *Every hour I need thee!*
> *Bless me now, My Savior,*
> *I come to thee.*[5]

The woman with the issue of blood reminds us that the path to the miraculous begins when we recognize our spiritual poverty apart from God and refuse to be satisfied in that state. Her desperate condition would not have changed if she had not coupled it with raw determination to get close to Jesus. Our own change depends upon the same.

Heavenly Father,

I am lost without You! I am humbled and amazed by the way that You have lifted me up out of the darkness and bondage of sin and given me new life through Jesus Christ, Your Son. Never let me forget how helpless I am without You and at the same time how complete I am in You. Forgive me for the ways I have played the Pharisee, pleased with my own performance, when it is Your grace alone that justifies. Today, and every day, let me put my confidence in You.

In Jesus' name, amen.

Questions for Reflection

or Small Group Study

1. Read Ephesians 2:1–9. How does this passage remind us of where we came from, and how does that perspective shape our ongoing walk with God?

2. In what ways have you been like the Pharisee from Jesus's parable in Luke 18:9–14? In what ways have you been like the tax collector?

3. What if the woman with the issue of blood had not run out of her resources before hearing of Jesus? Do you think she still would have sought Him out, or would she have waited until she became even more desperate? How do we do the same?

4. Jesus said that those who are not sick do not need a physician (Mark 2:17). What roadblocks do you suppose keep people from recognizing their sicknesses and confessing their needs?

5. How easily do you suppose it is to drift away from our confidence in His righteousness and begin trusting in our own?

6. Read Philippians 3:3 and Galatians 6:14. Like Paul, we might be tempted to put our confidence in our religious performances or pedigrees. What might that look like in today's church? In your life?

7. How might we recognize, nurture, and express our need for God in the everyday stuff of life?

Chapter Two

A DETERMINED HEART

You gotta have the want-to. -Allan Oggs

I was standing in line with my teenage son, Joshua, at the state wrestling championship in Rochester, Minnesota. Joshua was doing okay, having a decent enough season to get the state invitation, and impressing his coaches with his teachable and consistently positive attitude. We were in line to meet Anthony Robles, who had recently won the 2010–11 NCAA individual wrestling championship in the 125-pound weight class. I had enough time while we waited—as everyone seemed to want a picture with him—to become acquainted with his story.

Anthony wasn't always great at wrestling. His freshman year in high school, he finished with a record of five wins and eight losses, placing him dead last in the Mesa, Arizona, city rankings. However, Anthony was not a quitter. Determined to excel, he began rigorous training, and in his sophomore year, he placed sixth in the state. He only got better. In his junior and senior years of high school, Robles won ninety-six straight matches, claimed two state championships, and finished high school with a record of 129 wins and just fifteen losses.

In college, Anthony was nationally ranked each year he competed, becoming a three-time Pac-10 champion and claiming the national championship in his weight class. He concluded his wrestling career at Arizona State University with a record of 122 wins and twenty-three losses, ranking eighth for the most matches won by an Arizona State wrestler in their school history. In 2012, he was presented the 2011 Most Courageous Athlete Award by the Philadelphia Sports Writers Association.

What I didn't tell you was that Anthony Robles was born with only one leg.

Think of all the reasons you have come up with over the years to convince yourself not to try things. You're too short. Too tall. Too skinny. Too fat. Too ugly. Too whatever. We dare not, so we do not. Anthony could have listened to all the naysayers who told him that he couldn't possibly be successful as a wrestler and that he should find something else to do that was, you know, more *appropriate* for his condition. Whatever that means. But Anthony refused to allow his limitations to limit him. He was determined to wrestle, and he was determined to do it well.

How about you?

Think for a moment of the ways we limit God by allowing our circumstances to dictate our responses rather than the truth of His immutable character. "Behold, I am the LORD, the God of all flesh. Is there anything too hard for Me?" (Jeremiah 32:27). That's a rhetorical question, but sometimes we act like it's not. He is able! What if we allowed our hopes to be bigger than our self-imposed or socially imposed restrictions? What if we saw our struggles not as obstacles but as opportunities? What if we really believed the words of Jesus, that with God, *all things are possible?* (Mark 9:23).

But here's the key. The secret to all things being

possible, according to Jesus, is that we must *believe*. Please understand. I am not talking about the power of positive confession here. There is far too much name-it-and-claim-it, blab-it-and-grab-it theology out there already. What I *am* talking about is the kind of faith that stands upon the promises of God and then acts in faith according to those promises. Faith that works is faith *that works*. It's not faith that wishes or even faith that dreams; it is faith that pursues with fierce determination the object of that faith: Jesus Christ Himself. The writer of Hebrews tells us that without faith it is impossible to please God, for "he who comes to God must believe that He is, *and* that He is a rewarder of those *who diligently seek Him*" (Hebrews 11:6, emphasis added). We will explore this verse in greater depth in the next chapter, but for now, let's focus on the way that our faith produces in us the determination of mind that drives us forward.

She Came Behind Him in the Press

The kind of raw determination that settles for nothing less than full healing or deliverance is played out in some wonderful biblical narratives. We see it in the way that Zacchaeus climbed a tree to get the attention of Jesus as He passed by (Luke 19:1–6). We see it in the boldness of Bartimaeus, who cried out, "Son of David, have mercy on me!" even as everyone around him told him to be quiet (Mark 10:46–52). We see it in the faith of a few close friends who tore apart a roof in order to get one sick man close to Jesus (Mark 2:1–12).

And we see it in the story of the woman with the issue of blood.

The Scriptures tell us that "when she had heard of Jesus, [she] came in the press behind, and touched his garment; for she said, 'If I may touch but his clothes, I shall be whole'" (Mark 5:27–28 KJV). I love the way this plays out because it illustrates two important truths about her faith, which can be instructive for us.

First, notice the motivation for her faith. *If I can just touch His clothes, I will be healed.* She had a made-up mind. She did not say to herself, *Maybe* I will be healed. *Perhaps* things will work out. No! She was determined, convinced, and fully persuaded. In praying for wisdom, James warns us, "Let him ask in faith, with no doubting, for he who doubts is like a wave of the sea driven and tossed by the wind. For let not that man suppose that he will receive anything from the Lord" (James 1:6–7). Too often, as James tells us later, we have not, because we ask not, or because we ask to satisfy our lusts rather than His will (4:2-4). Whatever this woman had heard about Jesus, it triggered in her a full persuasion that should she get to Him, she would not leave His presence the same. When we gather as believers to worship God, to hear the Gospel preached, and to minister to one another by the anointing and leading of the Spirit, we should come with the same earnest expectation.

Years ago, we sang a beautiful but short chorus that went like this:

> *I won't go home, the way I came, in Jesus' name!*
> *I won't be bound, oppressed, tormented, sick or*
> *lame. For the Holy Ghost of Acts is still the same.*
> *I won't go home, the way I came, in Jesus' name!*

Over the years, our expectations have changed and so have our songs. Instead of ushering us into the manifest presence of God, we often settle for songs that affirm our theological sensitivities or that simply make us feel good. And all too often, we really don't expect God to show up at all. We have created a turnstile Christianity, where people are herded in and out of services to make room for the next crowd. No one lingers. No one tarries. No one travails. And no one is changed. We can learn a lot from a woman who refused to be just another face in the crowd.

She pressed through.

That's the second important truth we need to take notice of. She didn't come to these faith-filled conclusions only to stay where she was. She got up, she made her way to and then through the crowd that surrounded Jesus. The Scripture says, "She came behind him in the crowd." That sounds simple enough. In fact, we might quickly move on before really taking the time to imagine what that must have been like. The King James Version calls it "the press." I think that is a great way to describe it. It certainly sounds more difficult now. Sure enough, the Greek word here means "crowd," but it can connote much more than a large entourage and can include the idea of a mob, a throng, or a rabble. In other words, this was no orderly parade. People were jostling one another, bumping and pushing to get a closer look, or maneuvering to get within earshot of the sage from Galilee. Getting close to Jesus was no easy task! This woman was not going to just stroll up and play tag. It would take effort, it would take resolve, and it would take much, much risk.

Mark E. Kennicott

RISK VERSUS REWARD

Two thousand years removed from these events, it is easy to overlook important social and religious norms of the times. We think nothing of it when Jesus begins talking with a Samaritan woman near Jacob's well (John 4:7). We miss the shock of the crowd when Jesus describes a young man asking for his inheritance before his father has even passed away (Luke 15:12). And in Mark 5, even if we appreciate the difficulty this woman faced in getting to Jesus through the violence and tumult of the crowd, we scarcely understand the risk she was taking to be there in the first place.

According to Leviticus 15:25–27, this woman's continual flow of blood rendered her *zabah*, a state of continual uncleanness that meant that anything or anyone she touched became unclean. Mark tells us that she had been in this condition *for twelve years*, turning her whole world upside down. If she was married before this condition began, she was almost certainly not married now, for she would not have been able to touch her husband, or be touched by her husband, for all those many years. As I mentioned in the first chapter, she had spent all her resources and was now in all likelihood living outside the city, perhaps even in a leper colony, forced to cry "Unclean!" anytime someone got dangerously close to touching her.

Can you imagine?

Living without the ability to touch another human being, without the ability to hold or be held. This not only underscores the desperate condition we explored in the previous chapter, it also illustrates the profound shift in her thinking that must have driven her through the crowd that day. Despite all the dangers, she pressed on. Despite her status as a social outcast, she pressed on. Despite the consequences that would certainly be severe if she was discovered, she pressed on. She had weighed the risks versus the reward, and she had decided what mattered most.

What holds you back? In church, when the music is playing, and the minister has made the altar call, we sit back and allow the silliest things to keep us in our seats. We think, *I will look weak*, or *People with think I am struggling*, and God forbid anyone should think those things about us!

During the worship service, we feel the tug of the Spirit to lift our hands in surrender to Him, and instead of doing so, we stop and look around first to see *who else* is lifting their hands. We can't be the only one doing something so ... you know ... public! Perhaps we feel the drawing of God's Spirit to walk down to the altar, to bow upon our faces and worship Him unashamed. But not in the middle of the worship service! Everyone will look! An inner voice says, *You'll just be going down there to be seen. That's pride. Just stay here, and stay humble.* And so you sit, arms crossed, while the Spirit speaks to someone else.

It's time to press through.

It's time to decide what matters most, and it's not our pride, our reputations, or our sense of spiritual dignity. That was the Pharisee we read about, standing smug while others went home justified. Driven by the realization that we need Him more than we need anything else and convinced that we will find Him only when we search for Him with all of our hearts, we let go of our spiritual pride and our constant sense of self-consciousness in order to be more God-conscious.

To become aware of and alive to His presence.

To worship Him unashamed.

To press through when others won't.

PRESSING THROUGH WHEN OTHERS WON'T

I was attending a Hillsong United concert some years ago and noticed that a large crowd had gathered around the platform at the front of the church, which I took as an invitation to worship at the altar.

I was mistaken.

I went to the front and lifted my hands, singing the worship song as a prayer of sorts directly to God. I don't want to oversell my spirituality here, but I really was focusing on the Lord and could sense the joy and warmth of His presence. In the midst of that, a woman tapped me on the shoulder and leaned in to say, "I came to hear them, not you."

I was speechless.

It had not occurred to me that some of the people around the altar (I guess to some of them it was simply a *stage*) were not worshippers, but groupies. Hillsong groupies. Maybe even Jesus groupies.

I refuse to be a groupie.

More recently, my wife and I visited an allegedly Spirit-filled church. I don't mean to be overly critical here, but being from a Pentecostal background, I expect a Pentecostal church to be, you know, *Pentecostal*. Generally speaking, it has been my experience that Pentecostal churches tend to have a more "open" expression of worship, what we have come to call "liberty." Don't get me wrong. My wife and I are not overly demonstrative. We don't hang from the chandeliers or run the aisles.

At least not on the first visit.

But seriously, we will raise our hands, we will pray aloud, and we will (brace yourself) *sing along.* But alas, it was not meant to be. Somewhere in the middle of the worship service, the youth pastor tapped on my wife's shoulder (we know he was the youth pastor because he identified himself as such) and asked her to tone down her worship.

You read that correctly. *Tone down her worship.*

It broke my wife's heart. I had not noticed the exchange, as I had been singing along, eyes closed, and hands raised, right beside her. At some point, I turned and noticed that she was crying, but the tears did not look like tears of joy. I asked her what was wrong, and she shared the details with me.

We left.

And no, we haven't been back.

At the time, I'll admit it, I was angry. But after I seethed for a good two and a half minutes, my mind instantly went to 2 Samuel 6, where I was reminded of Michal, David's wife and Saul's daughter, who watched David from her window as he worshiped God in the streets below and despised him for it (vs. 16). She could hardly contain herself and came out to meet him as he returned home to let him know just how upset she was. Her sarcasm was dripping when she said, "How glorious was the king of Israel today, uncovering himself today in the eyes of the maids of his servants, as one of the base fellows shamelessly uncovers himself!" (vs. 20).

David's reply is priceless. Rather than be shamed by his wife, he insists, "It was before the LORD, who chose me instead of your father and all his house, to appoint me ruler over the people of the LORD, over Israel. Therefore I will play before the LORD. And I will be even more undignified than this, and will be humble in my own sight. But as for the maidservants of whom you have spoken, by them I will be held in honor" (vv. 21–22). Michal had accused him of being naked, when in fact he was adorned in a linen ephod (v. 14). He had placed his kingly robes aside to worship the King of kings. To Michal, this was a disgrace.

To David, this was worship.

What follows is as profound as it is instructive. The next verse simply states, "Therefore Michal the daughter of Saul had no children to the day of her death" (v. 23).

A church that discourages unashamed praise is a barren church.

Too many churches have a style of worship that is a mile wide but only an inch deep. Like Ezekiel, God is calling us out into the deep, into "waters to swim in!" (Ezekiel 47:5). To be fair, there are many churches that are not like this, but it is sadly not uncommon to see churchgoers act as spectators rather than participators in worship. Before we left that I day, I took a moment and looked around. I saw most people (in a church with over five hundred attendees) sitting back as though they were an audience rather than a congregation. It seemed that they were there to be entertained, rather than being there to entertain the presence of the Lord.

Granted, one should not presume to know what is taking place in the heart of another simply by appearances. But at some point, the outside will be a pretty good indicator of what is happening on the inside. In thinking all of this through, I began to ask questions. When did corporate worship become a concert? When did this all become about us? When did we become more concerned about how others see us instead of how God sees us? I appreciate good singing and skillful music, but it seems that the focus has shifted from the heart to the art, and we are unaware of the emptiness of it all. We will remain barren until we begin to sing, and to worship, and to pray for the audience of One. If we do not, we will be like those who surrounded Jesus as He walked, satisfied only to be in His presence, but unchanged by His power. A. W. Tozer said it well:

> When the Holy Spirit of God comes among us with His anointing, we become a worshiping people. This may be hard for some to admit, but when we are truly worshiping and adoring the God of all grace and of all love and of all mercy and of all truth, we may not be quiet enough to please everyone.[6]

Should everyone raise their hands, or weep openly, or sway under the Spirit for us to believe that they are worshiping God in spirit and in truth? No, of course not. I don't pretend to judge the way that men and women of different temperaments, cultural and religious upbringing, or social conditioning should respond to the presence of God. Only God knows the heart. I fear, however, that we may use this kind of rationale to excuse ourselves from being engaged in true heart worship. It may be true that *"it ain't all in the shouting,"* but it is also true that *"it ain't all in the sitting, either."*

Who Touched Me?

For the woman in our story, determination was met by deliverance. The moment she touched Jesus, she knew within herself that she had been healed. But before she could disappear into the crowd and slip away unnoticed, something else happened. Jesus stopped dead in His tracks and asked, "Who touched me?"

This is almost too good. Even the disciples were scratching their heads. This must have been more than a casual question because everyone quickly went into denial mode. "Not me!" was the knee-jerk response of everyone around. Then Peter spoke up, asking the obvious question, "Master, the multitudes throng and press You, and You say, 'Who touched Me?'" (Luke 8:45). "C'mon, Jesus," Peter seems to be saying, "Who touched You? Everyone is touching You!" But not everyone had touched Him in such a way that they were forever changed by the encounter.

People attend church week after week, sometimes for a lifetime, and engage with Jesus on merely the same level as the crowd that day. They enjoy being around

Him. They like rubbing shoulders with Him. They may even express some level of devotion to Him. But to allow Him to change them at the core of their beings? That's something altogether different. What this dear woman can teach us today is that there is a huge difference between being in the presence of Jesus and being in the place in His presence where virtue flows.

Jesus knew the difference.

He dismissed the incredulity of Peter's question and said, "Somebody touched Me, for I perceived power going out from Me" (Luke 8:46). Jesus knew what had happened, and He refused to allow this woman to slip away unnoticed. Her story had to be told. Her hope had to be restored. In seeking her out, Jesus ensured both.

Trembling, the woman came and fell before Him. She knew what she had done. She knew the risk she had taken. Had she touched Him, only to remain in her condition, the crowd would have become a mob. Everyone she had touched, having been defiled by her blood, would have been shouting for blood. But instead, something beautiful happened. Instead of her uncleanness making Jesus unclean, His purity made her pure. Her situation was changed by His sufficiency. Her problem was met by His power.

After her confession, Jesus simply said, "Daughter, be of good cheer; your faith has made you well. Go in peace" (Luke 8:48). He could have berated her, but He blessed her instead. How instructive. I've heard people say over the years, "I can't come to your church. I am such a sinner that if I walk in, the walls will fall down." There must be a movie with that line in it somewhere because I have heard it on more than one occasion. But such an attitude underestimates the cleansing power of God's holiness and grace. In the presence of Jesus, a woman's uncleanness became cleanness. Jesus did not call her out to run her off, but to comfort her and instruct those of us who would read her story. Come to church as you are, and *walls will fall*, but not the walls you think. God's grace has a way of reaching you where you are.

The Blessings of Persistence

When Allan Oggs was born in late September 1935, doctors told his parents that he would never walk, or talk, or even see. Diagnosed with severe cerebral palsy, a disorder that affects muscle tone, movement, and motor skills, the future looked bleak. But God had other plans for Allan, and as time would tell, he didn't care what he was not supposed to be able to do. Graduating from high school in 1955, Oggs felt the call of God upon his life, and so he attended, and later graduated, from Bible college. He would spend the remainder of his life—over fifty years—preaching the Gospel, pastoring churches, training ministers, and encouraging others. His enduring work is in the lives that he touched and in the books that he wrote. For years he travelled and preached, sharing his testimony, usually with a case or two of perhaps his most famous book, *You Gotta Have the Want To*. He eventually captured the attention of Dr. James Dobson, who invited him to share his story on the nationally broadcasted radio show *Focus on the Family*.

His book title really says it all.

Like the woman with the issue of blood teaches us, a determined heart will create a persistent and passionate pursuit. It will instill within us *the want-to*, the inner drive that will not let us rest until we reach out and lay hold of the prize.

Blessings await those who will not allow themselves to be distracted. Paul wrote, "I press toward the goal for the prize of the upward call of God in Christ Jesus" (Philippians 3:14). He admonishes us, "Therefore let us, as many as are mature, have this mind" (v. 15). I like the way this is rendered in The Message: "So let's keep focused on that goal, those of us who want everything God has for us." Amen!

When it comes right down to it, in order to have the want-to, in order to press through and lay hold of the good things of God, we need to have a made-up mind. We need to have decided, like the woman with the issue of blood, where the prize lies. For Paul, it was also clear. "*That I may know Him* and the power of His resurrection, and the fellowship of His sufferings, being conformed to His death, if, by any means, I may attain to the resurrection from the dead" (Philippians 3:10–11, emphasis added).

He is the prize.

David felt the same way, writing, "*One thing* I have desired of the LORD, that will I seek after: that I may dwell in the house of the LORD all the days of my life, To behold the beauty of the LORD, and to inquire in His temple" (Psalm 27:4, emphasis added).

The determination to press through and lay hold grows out of the place where a desperate need meets a daring faith, and it is to the latter we now turn.

PRAYER

Lord Jesus,

How many times have I been satisfied to be in Your presence but unwilling to be changed by Your power? How many services have I attended, missing a divine encounter, simply because I lacked the resolve to press through? Forgive me, O Lord! Stir within me a greater passion for Your presence and a holy discontentment that will not be satisfied with anything less than Your very best for me. Help me press through even when others won't, to worship You in Spirit and in truth, and to desire You even more than anything You might do for me. You are the prize!

In Jesus' name, amen!

QUESTIONS FOR REFLECTION

OR SMALL GROUP STUDY

1. Consider the crowds that surrounded Jesus as He walked through the cities and villages of His day. How might the crowds in our churches today be similar? How might they be different?

2. Read Isaiah 12:6. What would it look like today if our worship experience reflected this kind of proclamation?

3. How does the barrenness of Michal (2 Samuel 6:23) speak to our current culture of worship?

4. Read Mark 6:1–6. In what ways might we also limit the miraculous ministry of Jesus in our midst due to our familiarity with Jesus, our expectations, or lack thereof?

5. What would pressing through look like in today's church? What hindrances need to be overcome?

6. Read 1 Thessalonians 5:19–21 and discuss ways to apply it in your current worship context.

7. How does the woman with the issue of blood inspire you to approach Jesus today?

Chapter Three

A DARING FAITH

It's the Him in the garment that makes all the difference.

There is a lot of talk about faith these days, and rightly so because the Scriptures say a lot about it, and so did Jesus. Unfortunately, faith in our times has been transformed in many circles into a magical ingredient that makes all your wishes come true, reducing God to the genie in the bottle who promises to give you all that you desire *if you just believe.* And of course, we are often encouraged to prove our belief with some kind of monetary gesture. "If you give," they say, "you'll get."

Your "faith seed" is guaranteed to produce a harvest of blessings, just so long as you sow it in the right field. *Their field.*

As you can guess, I am not a fan of the prosperity gospel. In fact, I am convinced that the prosperity gospel turns the message of the Cross on its head and turns faith into nothing more than a cleverly veiled form of idolatry. A gift meant to fix our eyes on Christ somehow becomes a lens through which we see *ourselves* as the object of our faith. But make no mistake, a faith that leads us away from the Cross *is not the faith of the Bible.* The prosperity gospel teaches people to put their faith *in faith* and to make possessions, not a person, the pursuit of that faith. It suggests that we can twist God's arm to do our bidding, when seeking Him should position us—by faith—to do *His* will and to live according to *His* purpose, *not ours.*

Can I ruffle some feathers?

Jesus didn't teach His disciples to pray the prayer of Jabez; He taught them to pray, "*Your* kingdom come, *Your* will be done, on earth as it is in heaven" (Matthew 6:10, emphasis added). Jabez wanted more land; I don't know about you, but what I want is *more of Jesus.* A. W. Tozer said it this way:

Much is being said of faith these days that is not the focus of the Scriptures. We must shun all ways contrary to Scripture. Faith is not the key to get you what you want. Faith is not some magical formula that no matter who uses it, saved or unsaved, God has to act upon it. Such is religious lunacy and borders on witchcraft. I firmly believe that true faith rises in the soul of the man or woman who will fall on his face before an open Bible and allow God to be God in his life.[7]

Amen!

Now make no mistake about it, Jesus *did* teach His disciples, and us by extension, to pray in faith. He said, "If you believe, you will receive whatever you ask for in prayer" (Matthew 21:22). On the face of it, that seems to argue against everything above. The problem is that this verse cannot be understood in isolation. We need to put it back into the immediate context of Jesus's teaching, and then into the broader context of Matthew's Gospel, and then into the even wider context of the whole counsel of God's Word. Only when we allow this saying to be understood in that light can we make sense of such a wonderful invitation to pray and avoid the pitfalls of the prosperity gospel's error.

In the immediate context, Jesus uses the withering of the fig tree (Matthew 21:18-20) to teach His disciples about praying with confidence. Preceding the verse above, He tells His disciples, "Truly I tell you, if you have faith and do not doubt, not only can you do what was done to the fig tree, but also you can say to this mountain, 'Go, throw yourself into the sea,' and it will be done" (Matthew 21:21). Interestingly, the word translated as "doubt" here is different from the word used in Matthew 14:31 and 28:17 and speaks of *hesitation* and *double-mindedness*.

The kind of doubt that Jesus is discouraging is not doubt about your faith, but doubt *about your God.*

The writer of Hebrews tells us to "approach God's throne of grace *with confidence,* so that we may receive mercy and find grace to help us in our time of need" (Hebrews 4:16, emphasis added). One translation renders the Greek word for *confidence* as *boldness,* which is not bad, so long as we know what that boldness is rooted in. Our boldness before the throne has nothing to do with any merit of our own, which includes the force of our own faith, as though God should do things for us simply because we believe it hard enough. No, our confidence is rooted in His goodness, not ours. Our faith rests in His character, not ours. That is what Hebrews 4 emphasizes in verses 14–15, that our access to God is built on the high priestly empathy of Jesus Christ, who "was tempted in every way, just as we are, but did not sin" (v. 15). The doubt that Jesus wants us to avoid in our prayers and petitions is the kind that doubts God's power or that doubts His willingness to respond.

It was in this same sense that James encouraged his readers to ask God for wisdom, without doubting. The confidence of faith that James is encouraging is based on the character of God, "who gives generously to all without finding fault" (James 1:5–7). Likewise, the prayers Jesus promises to answer are not whatever-you-want kind of prayers, but whatever-you-ask in agreement with His will, trusting in the goodness and sovereignty of God. Jesus modeled that kind of prayer for us in Gethsemane (Matthew 26:39), reminding us that the prayer of faith should align us with God's purposes and promises, regardless of our personal wishes for comfort or blessing.

Focusing on the word for doubt in the text above

may seem like a diversion from the plain promise of the Scripture. I understand that. But in order to paint a picture of what praying in faith *is*, it is helpful to paint a picture of *what it is not*. From Jesus's own emphasis on praying without doubt, we can see that our faith—the kind of faith that moves mountains—is not faith in faith, but faith rooted in the goodness and willingness of God to act in accordance with His Word.

FAITH THAT WORKS

So what kind of faith is faith that works? Returning to Hebrews, we can see a wonderful definition of biblical faith:

> But without faith it is impossible to please Him, for he who comes to God must believe *that He is, and that He is a rewarder of those who diligently seek Him."* (Hebrews 11:6, emphasis added)

From this text, we can see that at the heart of faith is two inseparable ideas—that *God is real* and that *God is good;* that He is there and that He is reachable; that He knows and that He cares. Biblical faith is not believing in the power of our prayers, but believing in the power of the One we connect with in prayer. The distinction is crucial. Without it, we depersonalize God and turn Him into a cosmic grab bag, a heavenly vending machine. But true faith is rooted in the reality of God's personal care for His people.

He is, and He is a rewarder of those who diligently seek Him.

Faith that works is faith that puts its confidence *in the One* who saves, and delivers, and heals. It is faith that sees beyond the natural and perceives the supernatural. It is faith that rests in God's promises, and it is faith *that acts on God's promises*. That is what the second half of Hebrews 11:6 teaches us. It helps us see that biblical faith, the kind of faith that pleases God, is faith that responds to the reality of God by seeking Him out, by straining forward, like Paul, to lay hold of the prize (Philippians 3:14). That is the kind of faith that we see in the story of the woman with the issue of blood, and it is to her story that we now return.

If I Can Just Touch His Clothes

In our story, we get just a glimpse of the woman's faith when she thinks, *If only I may touch His clothes, I shall be made well* (Matthew 9:21). That's all we get, but it's enough. Granted, we will have to use our hermeneutic imagination a little, but stay with me here. Remember, this woman had a desperate need. We laid that foundation in Chapter One, and in the last chapter we explored the determination that drove her to press through the crowd. In all honesty, that is where we really see her faith played out. Her determination was fueled by her faith, just as her faith was demonstrated through her determined action. She believed something about Jesus that compelled her to diligently seek Him.

Let's consider Hebrews 11 again, but this time the entire chapter, as it has been called the *Faith Hall of Fame*. It begins with, "Now faith is confidence in what we hope for and assurance about what we do not see" (Hebrews 11:1). As we read down through all forty verses, we see faith lived out through extraordinary deeds, unshakable confidence, and unyielding hope. From these descriptions, it is reasonable to conclude that faith *in the unseen* is not necessarily faith *that is unseen*. The object of our faith may be unseen, as is our confidence and assurance, but the working out of that faith is clearly visible.

James said it like this: "Faith that you only talk about,

that you don't actually live out, isn't really faith at all." That's a paraphrase of all of James 2, which he concludes, "As the body without the spirit is dead, so faith without deeds is dead" (v. 26). For our faith to be genuine, it needs to be expressed by our actions. From James's perspective, faith has hands, and faith has feet. Faith is not dormant; faith is active.

Our woman in need did not possess a kind of passive faith that simply speculated on the ability of Jesus to heal her, otherwise we would have never heard of her, because she would have never moved. She could have believed all day long that Jesus was a great healer, but until she acted on that belief, until she got out of her bed and pressed through the crowd, her condition remained unchanged. But she was convinced that if she could just get to where Jesus was, *something would happen*. That cannot be called dormant faith, but can only be called *daring faith*.

It is daring faith that believes that God will do what He has promised that He will do.

It is daring faith that stares down a giant with a sling and a stone.

It is daring faith that gets out of the boat when Jesus says, "Come."

It is daring faith that tears a hole in a roof just to get one sick man close to Jesus.

It is daring faith that takes a lame man by the hand and lifts him up "in the name of Jesus."

It is daring faith that boldly proclaims the Gospel in front of the Sanhedrin, that sings praises to God in prison, and that remains calm in shipwreck.

That is not passive faith; that is daring faith!

Daring to Believe

Of course, these are all biblical examples, but what about today? Do you believe that God does today what He did back then? Does God still act in supernatural ways, or has the new Trinity become the Father, the Son, and the Holy Bible? I say this tongue-in-cheek, but the reality is that many Christians feel nervous about the ministry of the Holy Spirit today, and some even deny that the Spirit remains active at all, since we now have the full canon of Scripture. But having the Scriptures does not mean that we no longer need the Spirit. To the contrary, *it is the witness of the Scriptures that very clearly promises us the ministry of the Spirit!* Spirit and truth are not mutually exclusive; in fact, the Holy Spirit is called the Spirit of

Truth (John 14:17). The reason that so many Christian leaders shy away from the ministry and manifestation of the Spirit is because the Spirit is not easily controlled. Like Aslan in *The Chronicles of Narnia*, the Spirit—which is God Himself—is good, but *He is not safe*. The Holy Spirit will mess with your agenda. The Holy Spirit, like the wind, moves where He wills (John 3:8), and all we can do is recognize the Spirit's work. We cannot control it.

In Jesus's day, it was a common Jewish belief that the Holy Spirit had left Israel after the death of the last prophets,[8] in the same way that some Christians now believe that spiritual gifts ceased after the death of the last apostles. The Jews had the canon of the Hebrew Scriptures, and their focus became living by its precepts. Sounds familiar, doesn't it? Then along came Jesus and messed with everyone's comfortable theology. The Old Testament, Jesus taught, pointed to Him and the work He would do, ushering in a new era of the Spirit as part of the in-breaking kingdom of God.

The New Testament canonizes this new reality. The fact is, the Old Testament looked forward in faith to Jesus, and the New Testament points back in faith to the same. But we must be careful not to suppose that the Bible simply delivers propositions to affirm; it does so much more, by supplying *promises to appropriate.* At the risk of sounding heretical, let me point out that Jesus didn't come to give us the Word (He was the Word incarnate!); *He came to give us the Spirit.* Jesus said, "Whoever believes in me, as Scripture has said, rivers of living water will flow from within them. By this he meant the Spirit, whom those who believed in him were later to receive" (John 7:38-39). I'll have more to say on this in the next chapter, but for now I want to emphasize that the woman with the issue of blood could have allowed the current views of skepticism regarding the miraculous to prevent her from seeking Jesus out, but she did not.

She dared to believe.

Today, I wonder if the reason we do not experience the miraculous in our own churches, communities, or lives is because we have not dared to believe. Again, I am not talking about magic formulas or guaranteed results. God is sovereign! But He has made promises, and He invites us to pray in faith, believing that what He has promised, He is able and willing to perform. We have a choice. We can either affirm His promises, or we can relegate them to the distant past, convinced that "that was then, and this is now." It was Rolfe Barnard who once said, "One of these days someone is going to come along and pick up a Bible and believe it—and put the rest of us to shame."[9] So instead of reading about the way that God moved in the Scriptures and saying, "That was then, and this is now," daring faith says, "That was then, and *why not now?*"

Perhaps "daring" faith creates a false impression that there is any other kind. Biblical faith is nothing less than daring! But it is also an informed faith, faith that is rooted in *God's person* just as much (if not more so) as it is in *God's promises*. For the woman with the issue of blood, this was true as well. In the rest of this chapter, I want to unpack my conviction that her daring faith was rooted in both. I believe that she was convinced that she would be made whole because of *who Jesus was* just as much as she believed in *what He could do*. In fact, I think it is fair to suppose that what she believed He *could do* was based on *who she believed He was*. The question that then arises is, what did she know, and how did she know it? We will have to speculate a little, but there are two clues in the text that help point us in the right direction, the first regarding what she heard, and the second regarding what she did as a result.

Hearing About Jesus

Without any detail or elaboration, the Bible simply says that "when she heard about Jesus, she came up behind him in the crowd and touched his cloak" (Mark 5:27). We do not know what she heard, or who she heard it from, but we do know that she heard about Jesus, and what she heard was enough to inspire the kind of faith that caused her to press through the crowd to touch Him. I mentioned earlier that her condition would have made her a social outcast. She would not be able to get the daily news or local gossip at the well or in the market, like most others. She lived an isolated life, among other outcasts. She was an untouchable, and so she lived among other untouchables.

The amazing thing is, Jesus spent a great deal of His time in ministry touching the untouchables. Matthew writes, "Jesus went through all the towns and villages, teaching in their synagogues, proclaiming the good news of the kingdom and healing every disease and sickness" (Matthew 9:35). When others shunned the outcasts, Jesus sought them out. He was known as "a friend of tax collectors and sinners" (Matthew 11:19).

When others were concerned about hand-washing rituals, Jesus was getting His hands dirty, bringing hope and healing to people the world would not touch with a ten-foot pole. Surely this kind of news would spread! One of the first miracles recorded in Mark's Gospel illustrates this well:

> A man with leprosy came to him and begged him on his knees, "If you are willing, you can make me clean." Jesus was indignant. He reached out his hand and touched the man. "I am willing," he said. "Be clean!" Immediately the leprosy left him and he was cleansed. Jesus sent him away at once with a strong warning: "See that you don't tell this to anyone. But go, show yourself to the priest and offer the sacrifices that Moses commanded for your cleansing, as a testimony to them." Instead *he went out and began to talk freely, spreading the news.* As a result, Jesus could no longer enter a town openly but stayed outside in lonely places. Yet the people still came to him from

everywhere. (Mark 1:40–45 NIV, emphasis added)

This is a textbook example of someone who was considered untouchable. A person with leprosy was obliged to avoid the crowds and to warn them of his or her condition by shouting "Unclean!" so that they would keep their distance. If there were ever a case where healing from a distance would be preferred, this was it. Jesus proved on another occasion that He could do just that,[10] so why not now?

Perhaps it as precisely because this man *needed to be touched.* The NIV rendering, "Jesus was indignant" may not be the best translation, as others describe Jesus as being "moved with compassion," (NKJV, NLT, NASB, HCSB), "moved with pity" (ESV, NRSV), "deeply moved" (Message), and "moved with pity and sympathy" (Amplified). Jesus looked beyond the condition *and saw the man.* He saw a man whose life had been shattered by isolation and rejection. If He *was* indignant, it was not toward the man, but toward the wretched condition that kept this man in bondage.

In the culture of the first century, and especially

among the religious elite, a victim of leprosy was often believed to have been afflicted by God. It was assumed that his or her disease resulted from some sin, attitude, or choice that deserved just punishment, and one of God's chief tools for administering justice was the infliction of this debilitating, humiliating, and miserable disease.[11]

Reaching out to touch the leper would do more than provide physical healing; it would demonstrate that this man was no longer an outsider, no longer afflicted by God, no longer rejected, *no longer untouchable.* As the nerves that had been deadened by the ravages of leprosy came alive again by the simple touch of Jesus, this man's senses awakened. It was like coming back from the dead. He was restored to life, restored to God, and restored to the world.

Imagine with me what you would do next if it had been you. I think your story would read a lot like his. Jesus told him to go and make the appropriate sacrifice and to keep quiet about it. Instead, he went out and began to talk freely, spreading the news. Yup, that's what I would do; that's what you would do. We'd tell everyone! Like this man, we'd go places we couldn't go before,[12] see people we previously had to avoid, and enjoy life in ways that we thought were distant memories.

When I think about what the woman with the issue of blood had heard about Jesus, this is the kind of story that comes to mind. She lived among the very people that Jesus was in the habit of healing. Reports of so-and-so who crossed paths with Jesus and got to go home to his or her family made her come alive with hope and expectation. Sure, she could believe the reports of the naysayers who accused Jesus of peddling in demonic power (Mark 3:22), or she could believe the reports of those who saw Jesus cast out demons, while they confessed, "You are the Son of God!" (Mark 3:11). Better yet, she may have heard reports from the very people who had previously been demonized, as they shared their stories with anyone who would listen.

Whose report will you believe?

THE HEM OF HIS GARMENT

Beyond what we are told about the woman hearing about Jesus, we are told specifically what she wanted to do as a result. Her faith was undoubtedly stirred by the reports of all that Jesus was doing, but there was more to it than that. Speculation about who this man from Galilee was surrounded every report about His deeds. "Some say that you are John the Baptist, some say that you are Elijah, and others say maybe Jeremiah or one of the prophets" (Matthew 16:14, paraphrase). You could not talk about what Jesus did without the conversation leading to questions about who Jesus was. Again, we do not know exactly what the woman with the issue of blood thought about Jesus, but there are clues that point us in the right direction.

The Bible says that she said within herself, "If I just *touch his clothes*, I will be healed" (Mark 5:28). The clue here is in *which part* of His clothes she wanted to touch. Mark simply says she touched "His cloak" (Mark 5:27), but both Matthew and Luke tell us that she touched "*the edge* of His cloak" (Matthew 9:20; Luke 8:44), what the King James Version calls "*the hem*" (in Matthew), or "*the border*" (in Luke) of His garment.

In both Matthew and in Luke, the Greek word is the same and literally means *the fringe* or *tassel* on the corner of His cloak. Observant Jewish men in Jesus's day wore tassels on the four corners of their garments in obedience to Numbers 15:37–41 and Deuteronomy 22:12:

The L<small>ORD</small> said to Moses, "Speak to the Israelites and say to them: Throughout the generations to come you are to make tassels on the corners of your garments, with a blue cord on each tassel. You will have these tassels to look at and so you will remember all the commands of the L<small>ORD</small>, that you may obey them and not prostitute yourselves by chasing after the lusts of your own hearts and eyes. Then you will remember to obey all my commands and will be consecrated to your God. I am the L<small>ORD</small> your God, who brought you out of Egypt to be your God. I am the L<small>ORD</small> your God." (Numbers 15:37–41)

Make tassels on the four corners of the cloak you wear. (Deuteronomy 22:12)

These tassels, called *tzitzit,* consisted of four strands of wool folded over through a slit in the garments' corner and knotted. The garment as a whole was called a *tallit.* Today they are worn primarily for synagogue worship or on a specially made undergarment called a *tallit katan*, a "*little tallit*." In Jesus's day, however, the *tzitziyot* (plural) were attached to the four corners of the outer garment, what is called in Scripture a *cloak* or a *mantle*. They were commanded to be worn as a reminder of God's commandments, a visual cue that the people of Israel were a royal priesthood, a nation in covenant with God.

People often do not envision Jesus wearing this garment, since paintings and movies usually depict only the Pharisees or members of the Sanhedrin in such attire. This has unfortunately caused a lot of people to misunderstand the relationship that Jesus had with the Law, supposing that at every turn He was undermining the commandments of Moses, when in fact He said that He did not come to abolish the Law, but to fulfill it (Matthew 5:17). However, Jesus did criticize those who turned the obedience of these commandments into an outward show, as He did in Matthew 23:5 with regard to these very tassels in His criticism of the Scribes and Pharisees:

> Everything they do is done for people to see: They make their phylacteries wide and the tassels on their garments long.

Still, these tassels were not only worn by Jesus, but are also prominent features of Old Testament stories that you may be familiar with. When Saul tried to prevent Samuel from leaving after God had rejected him, the Bible says, "Saul caught hold of the hem of his robe, and it tore" (1 Samuel 15:27). The Hebrew word for *hem* here is *kanaph* and refers to the corner of the garment where the tassels were attached. In reaching out to stop Samuel, Saul tore a *tzitzit* off Samuel's cloak. This was significant because the *tzitziyot* on the cloaks of prophets, priests, and kings were symbolic of their spiritual authority.[13] By tearing Samuel's robe in this way, Saul symbolically invalidated Samuel's authority. But Samuel used it as an object lesson for the way that God had invalidated Saul's authority as king of Israel (v. 28).

These tassels are also important later when David has an opportunity to kill Saul while he is sleeping, but does not. Instead, the Bible says he "crept up unnoticed and cut off a corner of Saul's robe" (1 Samuel 24:4). The Scripture reports that David was "conscience-stricken" for doing this (v. 5), and although the text does not tell us why, we may surmise that it is precisely because of what this action represented.

David had symbolically *assaulted the king's authority to reign*, an action "tantamount to knocking the crown off Saul's head, a job David believed belonged only to the Almighty."[14]

Perhaps my favorite mention of the *tallit* in the Old Testament comes from the narrative of 1 Kings 19, where Elijah throws his mantle on Elisha, in effect calling him into the ministry (v. 19–21). Because of all that the *tallit* represented, this was no insignificant gesture! It was a way of saying, "I am going to share my anointing and authority with you." No wonder Elisha left everything to follow him!

Years later, when Elijah was taken up from Elisha in a chariot and a whirlwind, the Scriptures tell us that Elijah's mantle (his *tallit*) fell to the ground, and that Elisha took it in his hands (perhaps holding it by the four corners?) and struck the Jordan, saying, "Where now is the LORD, the God of Elijah?" (2 Kings 2:11–14). Doing this, the waters parted, and Elisha crossed over.

HEALING IN HIS WINGS

Taking into consideration all that the *tallit* represented in biblical times—and specifically, the *tzitziyot*—it begins to make sense why the woman with the issue of blood would want to touch it. But once again, there is more. As I mentioned above, the corner of the cloak is known as the *kanaph*. Interestingly, it can also be translated as "wing." David uses this word when he writes, "How priceless is your unfailing love, O God! People take refuge in the shadow of your wings (*kanaphim*)" (Psalm 36:7). Therefore, the four corners of the *tallit* are known as the *wings* of the garment. This is significant because a well-known Messianic text of Jesus's day was Malachi 4:2, which says:

> But to you who fear My name The Sun of Righteousness shall arise *with healing in His wings.* (emphasis added)

This may be the most significant verse we can turn to in order to understand what the woman with the issue of blood thought about Jesus as she pressed through the crowd. Taking our cue from Malachi, it seems that it was the *Him in the garment,* and not the *hem of the garment,* that made all the difference in the world for this desperate woman. It is likely that every man in the crowd that day had tassels hanging from his cloak, but only Jesus could be called the *Sun of Righteousness!*

PRESSING THROUGH TODAY

The motivation behind the daring faith of the woman with the issue of blood may be impossible for us to know with certainty, but the clues within the text help us make sense of her resulting determination and give us a solid grounding for our own spiritual journeys. If we are going to demonstrate the same kind of daring faith, it must begin with the conviction that *He is God, and He is good!* Our confidence must be rooted in the character of God, grounded in the promises of Scripture, and nurtured by the testimony of others who have experienced His goodness. *Be careful who you listen to.* Believing that God can do today what He has done before does not mean that we should expect the exact same thing the exact same way, since God does not always do a repeat performance, nor is He obligated to do so. *We cannot put God in a box.* However, it does mean that we should pray in faith, expect the same God to show up, and invite Him to do so *in a big way.* In order to press through today, we must believe that Jesus is who the Bible says He is, and we must believe that He continues to reward those who diligently seek Him. That is the only way for us to find ourselves in the place in His presence *where virtue flows.*

PRAYER

Lord Jesus,

I confess and declare that You are the same yesterday, and today, and forever, and there is nothing too hard for You! Forgive me for the ways that I have allowed doubt, discouragement, and complacency to quench my faith, to rob me of Your blessings, and to cause me to settle for less than Your very best. Prepare my heart now to receive with faith the promise of Your Word, the promise of power for all those who put their trust in You.

In Jesus' name, amen!

QUESTIONS FOR REFLECTION
OR SMALL GROUP STUDY

1. Read Proverbs 19:21 and James 4:3. Why is it so important for our faith in God to align with the Word of God and the will of God?

2. What might happen if we emphasized one of the two truths of Hebrews 11:6 to the neglect of the other? Why is it important that we affirm both the reality of God and the character of God as we seek Him?

3. How would you describe your faith? Daring? Dormant? In what ways is God leading you to put feet to your faith and live it out more decisively?

4. How does understanding the Jewishness of Jesus, specifically with regard to the part of the garment he wore, help you understand the story of the woman with the issue of blood?

5. What promises in God's Word have you been afraid to believe up until now? Do you sense that the Holy Spirit wants you to change your mind?

6. Read Matthew 8:16–17 and James 5:14–16. How does the prophecy of Malachi 4:2 still speak to us today?

7. What would have happened to the woman with the issue of blood had she not acted on her belief in who Jesus was? How does that inspire you today?

Chapter Four

AN ENDURING PROMISE

*For the promise is to you and to your children, and to all who are afar
off, as many as the Lord our God will call. Acts 2:39*

The woman with the issue of blood still speaks
to us today because we can relate so intimately with
her story. Her desperate need reminds us of our
brokenness and our inability to change on our own. Her
determination inspires us to press on and press through
despite what others may think and despite what others
might settle for. Her daring faith challenges us to trust in
God's character as much as in God's promises, believing

that He still rewards those who diligently seek Him. She reminds us that Jesus is willing and able to meet us at the point of our need and that His grace continues to be sufficient for us.

As we consider all the ways that this story might be applied to our lives today, there is an enduring promise that we have yet to explore but that is beautifully illustrated within the biblical narrative.

In the Introduction, I explained how the King James rendering of *virtue*, which inspired the title of this book, is translated in modern Bibles as *power*. When the woman with the issue of blood reached out and touched Jesus, He perceived that virtue, or *power*, had gone out of Him, making her whole. Having grown up reading and memorizing from the King James Version, I love the ring of the word *virtue*. Still, *power* is accurate. Simply reading *virtue*, it is easy to miss an important connection this story shares with another passage of Scripture, a passage that contains a beautiful promise.

When Jesus was about to ascend into heaven, leaving His disciples with the task of taking the Gospel to the far corners of the world, He instructed them to "tarry in the city of Jerusalem, until you are endued with *power* from on high" (Luke 24:49). The Greek word for power here, *dunamis*, speaks of *miraculous power*, the anointing that was upon Jesus and which would soon be upon His disciples. Peter would later testify "how God anointed Jesus of Nazareth with the Holy Spirit and with power [*dunamis*], who went about doing good and healing all who were oppressed by the devil, for God was with Him" (Acts 10:38).

This is the same word for power found in the story of the woman with the issue of blood. The power that flowed into her body, making her whole and restoring her life, is the same power that is available to us today through the baptism of the Holy Spirit. Like the woman with the issue of blood, we need only lay hold of the promise.

YOU SHALL RECEIVE POWER

According to the Scriptures, it was the anointing of the Holy Spirit that enabled Jesus to do the miraculous deeds that He did. Yes, He was (and is!) the incarnate Son of God, but He depended on the anointing of the Spirit, just as His disciples would, so that He could serve as our example (cf. Phil. 2:5–8; John 5:19). J. D. Greear writes:

If Jesus had healed exclusively out of his own power, then he'd have a significant advantage over his disciples. But if the Holy Spirit empowered Jesus, then the disciples could do what he did, continuing the ministry he started. Believers, who now possess that same Holy Spirit, have access to that *same power*.[15]

Having borne witness to the Gospel of the kingdom of God in His own ministry and nearing His departure, Jesus made it clear that His disciples would also need to depend on the anointing of the Holy Spirit to continue His work. That anointing would come in Jerusalem, when they would be endued (the NIV says "clothed") with power from on high (Luke 24:49).

The last words of Jesus in Luke are His first words in Acts. Once again, He reminds His disciples that they need to wait for the "promise of the Father" (Acts 1:4). Anticipating the restoration of Israel's kingdom, the disciples missed the point altogether, supposing that Jesus would now overthrow Rome and usher in the Messianic Age. But the Father, said Jesus, had other plans, pointing instead to an Age of the Spirit in which God's redemptive reign would spread through the preaching of the Gospel. To that end, Jesus said, "You shall receive *power* when the Holy Spirit has come upon you; and you shall be witnesses to Me in Jerusalem, and in all Judea and Samaria, and to the end of the earth" (v. 8). The baptism of the Holy Spirit, sent on the Day of Pentecost (Acts 2), would provide the ongoing power that the disciples would need to take the Gospel message to the ends of the earth. But that baptism was more than mere power; it was the culmination of prophetic promises. It was the beginning of the Age of the Spirit, or what some have called the Age of the Church.

Jesus made it clear that by the baptism of the Holy Spirit, the disciples would have the same empowerment for their mission that He had for His. However, there would be a difference. While the Scriptures tells us that Jesus had the Holy Spirit *without measure* (John 3:34), we, on the other hand, are "sealed with the Holy Spirit" (Ephesians 1:13–14). Our baptism, according to Paul, is a down payment of sorts until the return of Christ and the final redemption. We have the same Spirit, but *in measure*, rather than *without measure*, so that only together, as the body of Christ, can we truly reflect the glory of Christ, who is the head of the body, the church (Ephesians 4:15).

Secondly, the Spirit would not only empower us but would also testify of Jesus in His absence (John 15:26). In fact, it may be too strong to speak of Jesus's *absence*, since through the Holy Spirit, Jesus is essentially promising to be with the disciples still, but *in a whole new way*. Consider John 14:16-18:

> And I will pray the Father, and He will give you another Helper, that He may abide with you forever—the Spirit of truth, whom the world cannot receive, because it neither sees Him nor knows Him; but you know Him, for He dwells with you and will be in you. I will not leave you orphans; I will come to you.

Here, Jesus promises that the coming Spirit will, in a sense, be the continuing presence of Jesus Himself in His people. What a promise! With Jesus *physically* present, His ministry was limited to where He was at any point in time, but by the presence of His Spirit at work in and through His people, His presence and His power would be multiplied exponentially. No wonder Jesus could tell His disciples, "Most assuredly, I say to you, he who believes in Me, the works that I do he will do also; and *greater works than these* he will do, because I go to My Father" (John 14:12, emphasis added). It was not the *quality* of the works that would increase, but the sheer *quantity* of them would be greater, since the baptism of the Spirit would invest the power that was at work in Christ *in the heart of every believer!*

THE FORGOTTEN PROMISE

In many ways, the promise of the Father has become the forgotten promise of the church today. Sure, we read about the baptism of the Holy Spirit in Acts 2, 8, 10, and 19 and take note of the supernatural signs that accompanied the Spirit's work in the life of the early church, but somewhere along the line we have relegated these baptisms and manifestations to the past, expecting much less from God in our modern experience.

We have become like the entourage that followed Jesus, happy to rub shoulders with the Master, and maybe even to be named among His followers, but never quite finding ourselves in the place where virtue flows.

Why is that?

Why have we settled for less? Who told us to read the Scriptures and not expect God to do today what He has done before? Who told us that God would not continue to keep His promise? Who would stand to profit from a spiritually anemic church, one that has a form of godliness but denies the power thereof? Any thoughts?

Look, I am not one to give undue attention to Satan, but let's face it. If there is anyone who would love for the church to forget its powerful spiritual heritage and settle for a religious expression devoid of actual spiritual experience, it would be the devil.

We do not challenge the kingdom of darkness when the light of the Spirit has been diminished in our midst.

We do not break strongholds without the anointing.

We do not intimidate the enemy when we preach a Jesus we have heard about but do not know personally and powerfully. That didn't work out too well for the seven sons of Sceva (see Acts 19:13–16 for a colorful encounter!), and it continues to remind us that the Gospel is more than words, but includes a "demonstration of the Spirit and of power" (1 Corinthians 2:4).

Too many Christians today struggle with their day-to-day walk with God because they have been taught to pray a prayer, to shake a hand, and to "accept Christ," not understanding that the Gospel goes deeper than that. When Peter preached on the Day of Pentecost, letting every spectator know that the baptism of the Spirit they had seen and heard was the direct result of God's prophetic promises (cf. Acts 2:15–21; Joel 2:28–32) and that they had been guilty of crucifying the Lord of Life (Acts 2:26), they were cut to the heart. They asked, "Men and brethren, what shall we do?" (v. 37). Peter replied:

> Repent, and let every one of you be baptized in the name of Jesus Christ for the remission of sins; and you shall receive the gift of the Holy Spirit. For the promise is to you and to your children, and to all who are afar off, as many as the Lord our God will call. (Acts 2:38–39)

From Peter's perspective, the promise of the Spirit was not just for those few who were watching and waiting since the days after Jesus left. No, this promise was for *everyone*. It was the eschatological fulfillment of promises made long before in the Old Testament, and it was for "as many as the Lord our God will call."

He is still calling today!

THE REST OF THE STORY

One of my favorite radio broadcasters of all time has got to be Paul Harvey, whose news and comment filled the airwaves for over fifty years. In his *Rest of the Story* segments, he would share little-known anecdotes from the lives of historical or pop culture personalities, and in a final reveal, let you know who he was talking about. At the end of the story, he would say in his regal radio voice, "And now you know ... *the rest of the story!*"

When it comes to the Gospel, I fear that too many churches are only telling part of the story. Our focus on the finished work of Christ, which is essential to a biblical understanding of the Gospel, has led many churches to adopt an abbreviated presentation of propositions to be considered and confessed, rather than an invitation to receive all that God has promised. We press for decisions, when Jesus commissioned us to make disciples. We focus on what we can do and neglect the part that only God can do.

Maybe that is why the baptism of the Spirit, a

once-powerful experience accompanied by supernatural signs, has been replaced with short (and certainly sincere!) prayers to "invite Jesus into our hearts." Only God can pour out His Spirit. We've taken over and somehow edged the Spirit of God right out of the conversion process. Consider the words of Tozer, written over fifty years ago:

> If the Holy Spirit was withdrawn from the church today, ninety-five percent of what we do would go on and no one would know the difference. If the Holy Spirit had been withdrawn from the New Testament church, ninety-five percent of what they did would stop, and everybody would know the difference.[16]

What an indictment! What a change! How did we come to this place? And more importantly, how do we return to the focus and fire of that first church?

PARDON, PRESENCE, AND POWER

The church is not wrong to emphasize the pardon that Christ grants us through His sacrifice. But that is only part of the story. Paul writes that we were dead in our sins and that God made us alive in Christ, forgiving us (Colossians 2:13-14). We cannot, and dare not, minimize this truth. Placing our faith in Christ and trusting in the sufficiency of His sacrifice is a gift from God that brings us pardon, release, and wonderful depths of peace and joy. Make no mistake, salvation comes to those who call upon His name!

But here's the rest of the story. Jesus did not die to simply grant you His pardon; He died, and rose, and ascended to the right hand of the Father *to give you Himself!* In the baptism of the Spirit, Jesus promises to be with, and in, His people. He said it this way:

> O righteous Father! The world has not known You, but I have known You; and these have known that You sent Me. And I have declared to them Your name, and will declare it, that the love with which You loved Me may be in them, *and I in them."* (John 17:25-26, emphasis added)

As we read earlier, Jesus told His disciples that He would not leave them fatherless; *He would come to them.*

He said this just after describing the gift of the Spirit that they would receive at Pentecost! In Matthew's Gospel, Jesus concludes His commission by saying, "Lo, I am with you always, even to the end of the age" (Matthew 28:20).

Our contemporary telling of the Gospel is simply not complete if it does not include this aspect of God's redemptive purpose and promise. Jesus did not come simply to forgive us of our sins, as wonderful as that is. He came, even as John announced at the beginning of his ministry, to baptize us "with the Holy Spirit and fire" (Luke 3:16). He came to give us Himself, fully and forever.

But again, that's not all.

No, with the *pardon* that Christ provides and with the *presence* that He promises, He also gives us the *power* to serve Him effectively. We have already read the verses in Luke 14 and Acts 1 that make that clear, but what we might have missed are the implications of this truth.

First, Jesus makes it clear that the baptism of the Holy Spirit will empower us to proclaim Him in the world. We are His witnesses, and we are meant to engage in that witness through the power of the Holy Spirit. Unlike the Blues Brothers, we are not on a mission from God, we are on a mission *with* God. We are joining Him in His labors; we are coworkers with God (2 Corinthians 6:1).

Second, and this is crucial, the work of the Spirit is not simply something God does *through* us, it is also something that God does *in* us. In Ezekiel's prophecy of the outpouring of the Spirit, the Lord promises to give His people a new heart and a new spirit, to put His Spirit within them so that they might walk in His decrees and keep His laws (Ezekiel 36:25–27). The baptism of the Holy Spirit does more than empower us for witness; it imparts to us the nature of Christ and shapes us into His likeness, so that we might bear His fruit (Galatians 5:22–23) and demonstrate His glory (2 Corinthians 3:18).

The power of the Spirit is at work in us, making us more like Jesus, and that same power is at work through us, employing and energizing gifts to minister strength to His body and to minister healing and hope to the nations. Without the Spirit, Christianity becomes a works religion, where all we believe we need to do is try harder. But let's be clear—it's not about trying, it's about trusting. It's about drinking deeply from the well and sharing the life of Jesus as He gives it to us and lives it through us.

The pardon, presence, and power of Christ are all part of God's gift of grace and can be experienced by everyone who places their trust in Christ. But when it all comes down, many Christians live below this privilege, and for a very simple reason. They do not ask.

RECEIVING THE PROMISE

When Paul happened upon a group of disciples of John the Baptist in the city of Ephesus, he asked them an important question: "Did you receive the Holy Spirit when you believed?" (Acts 19:2). Today, that question seems superfluous, as we have been told over and over that every Christian receives the gift of the Spirit at the moment of conversion—that is, when they believe the Gospel message and place their faith in Christ.

How can Paul ask such a counterintuitive question?

Well, for starters, it made perfect sense to Paul. In the course of questioning, Paul discovered that these disciples only knew John's baptism and had not even heard that the baptism of the Spirit had begun in earnest, something that John predicted, but which did not take place until Pentecost. He redirected their faith, teaching them how John ultimately pointed people to Christ, and they were baptized again, only this time in the name of Jesus (v. 5). By this time, they believed the Gospel, and as a sign of their newly placed faith in Christ, they bore the seal of that faith by being baptized in water.

Still, something was missing.

Paul then laid his hands on them, and they were filled with the Holy Spirit, evidenced by speaking in tongues and prophesying (v. 6).

This beautiful passage illustrates an important truth about the baptism of the Spirit that eludes many Christians (and even some theologians) to this day. Conversion and Spirit baptism are *not necessarily* simultaneous in nature and may even be subsequent experiences. That is, a person may come to saving faith in Christ and even experience joy (see Acts 8:8) without actually receiving the gift of the Spirit.

We have been told that it is automatic, and even unconscious, so that we simply do not expect anything dynamic about the encounter, but that is a mistake.

Nobody received the baptism of the Holy Spirit in the New Testament on or after the Day of Pentecost who did not know it experientially.

In *Holy Fire: A Balanced, Biblical Look at the Holy*

Spirit's Work in Our Lives, R. T. Kendall shares some important insights on this subject that he gleaned from his long-time relationship with Dr. Lloyd-Jones. He writes:

> He [Dr. Lloyd-Jones] says over and over again that the sealing of the Spirit is a "conscious experience." He emphasized this because "most of the books which have been written on the Holy Spirit during the present [twentieth] century go out of their way to emphasize that the sealing of the Holy Spirit is not experiential, and has nothing to do with experience as such."[17]

Of course, if the baptism of the Spirit is completely nonexperiential, we need not concern ourselves. Again, we can lead people in prayer, slap them on the backs, and tell them, "You've got it!" as though just saying it, or believing it, were the same as having it.

The woman with the issue of blood could have just stayed home.

But no, there is a promise that we are meant to receive! A gift that we are meant to have! A power that we are meant to experience! The Gospel proclaims a God who is meant to be believed in *and encountered*. Tozer writes:

> It is not mere words that nourish the soul, but God Himself, and unless and until the hearers find God in personal experience, they are not the better for having heard the truth. The Bible is not an end in itself, but a means to bring men to an intimate and satisfying knowledge of God, that they may enter into Him, that they may delight in His presence, may taste and know the inner sweetness of the very God Himself in the core and center of their hearts.[18]

That is what God has prepared for those who put their trust in Him! And yet, why do so many Christians lack it? Why do believers give lip service to the power of the Spirit but make no room for it in their lives? It may well be because they have been told they have already received it the moment they believed and have simply not taken the time to evaluate their experience, or lack thereof, in light of what the Scriptures actually say. They lack the power and vitality of the Spirit, but they have been told that's all there is. They have not dared to believe, and so they have not dared to ask.

And James tells us that we have not, because we ask not (James 4:2). Still, the invitation of Jesus is clear:

> If anyone thirsts, let him come to Me and drink. He who believes in Me, as the Scripture has said, out of his heart will flow rivers of living water. (John 7:37b–38)

> If you then, being evil, know how to give good gifts to your children, how much more will your heavenly Father give the Holy Spirit to those who ask Him! (Luke 11:13)

Jesus is ready and willing to give anyone who is thirsty the gift of the Spirit. All you need to do is ask and believe that what God has promised, He is willing and able to do. *He will do it for you!*

WHAT TO EXPECT

Here is where things tend to get controversial. One cannot talk about an experiential encounter with

God without people asking, "Well, then, what should that experience look like?" How do we know that we have been baptized with the Holy Spirit if we are meant to recognize the event?

When God shows up, you will know it!

On the Day of Pentecost, signs that accompanied the baptism of the Spirit included the sound of a mighty rushing wind, visible tongues of fire, and speaking in other tongues "as the Spirit gave them utterance" (Acts 2:2–4). In Acts 8, signs are not mentioned, but something evidential is inferred by the fact that Simon the sorcerer was able to identify the baptism when it occurred (v. 17–19). In Acts 10, Cornelius and his household all received the baptism of the Holy Spirit, as evidenced by speaking in tongues and magnifying God (v. 46). And in Acts 19, when the disciples of John the Baptist received the Spirit, they spoke with tongues and prophesied (v. 6).

While all these passages paint a diverse picture, the only consistent sign of the baptism of the Spirit is speaking in tongues (except for Acts 8, where no sign is mentioned). *That is where things tend to get controversial, and a word of caution is in order.* While many reasonable theologians see speaking in tongues as an evidential sign of Spirit baptism in the book of Acts, a sign that continued (though scarcely) to manifest itself throughout church history, and a sign that has seen a powerful resurgence in the last century, they hesitate to suggest that it is *the only sign*. Still, the Scriptures make a compelling case for tongues as the *initial evidence* of Spirit baptism. Steve Bremner writes:

> An experience unique to the New Testament needs evidence that is also unique to the New Testament in order to know that they have received the New Testament experience of Spirit baptism. Any other evidence you can name to 'prove' they are baptized in the Holy Spirit happened in the Old Testament as well. Tongues didn't happen in the Old Covenant, so it is the only conclusive initial evidence we have to know that they have been baptized in the Holy Spirit at that moment.[19]

Questions regarding the nature and use of tongues usually surface based on mistaking the tongues in Acts with the tongues in 1 Corinthians 12–14. While they are the same in essence, they are clearly different in use and function. Even John R. W. Stott, who does not subscribe to the initial evidence doctrine, admits:

> In Acts *glossolalia* [tongues] seems to be evidential, an initial "sign" given to all, bearing witness to their reception of the Spirit, while in 1 Corinthians it is edificatory, a continuing "gift" bestowed on some for the building up of the church.[20]

People likewise get confused when it comes to Spirit baptism and tongues because they think they are meant to seek the "gift of tongues" as Paul describes it in 1 Corinthians 12–14. But this is not about the gift of tongues, which as Stott suggests is another matter altogether, but rather *the gift of the Spirit*, which is *accompanied* by tongues. The "sign gifts" that Paul describes are meant for specific people, places, and purposes, while tongues in general, like those we read about in Acts, are meant for every believer. Jesus may have even hinted at this when He said:

> The wind blows where it wishes, and you
> hear the sound of it, but cannot tell where
> it comes from and where it goes. So is
> everyone who is born of the Spirit. (John 3:8)

The People's New Testament Commentary says of this passage, "The Spirit breathes where it wills and you recognize its manifestation by *its voice*; by the words spoken by men of God as the Holy Spirit *gives them utterance*" (emphasis added).[21] On the Day of Pentecost, the people likewise recognized the manifestation of the Spirit's voice, as everyone who received the Spirit spoke with tongues "as the Spirit gave them utterance" (Acts 2:4). Just as a baby's cry is the sign of life in the natural, it seems that God has chosen tongues (*the voice of the Spirit*) to be the sign of life in the supernatural. This is true for "everyone who is born of the Spirit."

Can God fill a person with the Holy Spirit with some other sign? Is He not sovereign? These are rhetorical questions. Certainly He can, and certainly He is. But if just any sign or manifestation will do, then we have ceased to allow the Word of God to be the standard by which we evaluate our experience.

So what should we expect? While I have tried briefly to make a case for tongues as the initial evidence of Spirit baptism, and I truly expect to see that sign manifest whenever I pray with people to receive that precious gift, I am also not willing to put God in a box, and I suggest that you do not either. The Christian and Missionary Alliance, from whom I have received much of my formal religious education, offers the following position:

> A creed of power without the experience of power is worthless. One phrase that could describe our posture in this encounter with God is "Expectation without Agenda." It would seem to be a dangerous thing to try and convince someone they have been filled with the Spirit if there is no manifest evidence in their lives. Our expectancy should be that God will meet His people in a powerful way. However, it would be equally dangerous to demand a specific agenda or manifestation in that moment. Again, we should come to the Lord with

great expectation, while seeking to free ourselves from human agendas or motives.[22]

I appreciate that perspective. I do speak with tongues, and like Paul I want everyone else to do the same (1 Corinthians 14:5). I don't think that represents (as noted above) a human agenda or motive, but rather reflects an expectation based on God's revealed activity. Likewise, I do not *demand* a certain manifestation, but I have a confident expectation, based on the witness of the Scriptures, that God will use a specific sign to give evidence of His work. Nevertheless, the Alliance is right to suggest that we let God be God and to encourage our expectation that God would meet His people *in a powerful way*. Seeking for and receiving the baptism of the Holy Spirit should be our aim, not the pursuit of a particular manifestation.

There is a problem when the sign becomes the focus and not the gift itself. *We must be careful to seek the Holy Spirit and not tongues.* As we learned earlier, the gift Jesus invites us to seek is the gift of Himself, and our attention must therefore remain on Him. A. B. Simpson said, "When we seek anything less than God, we are sure to miss His highest blessing and likely to fall into side issues and serious errors."[23] I agree.

Do not seek tongues. Seek Jesus!

Do not seek signs. Seek Jesus!

Do not seek manifestations. Seek Jesus!

Surely, signs will follow those who believe, but things get out of kilter when it is the other way around and believers are following after signs. If we seek Jesus, we can be certain that He will not disappoint us. Like the woman with the issue of blood, when Jesus is the object of our faith and hope, we need only make our way to Him, and He will do the rest.

Pressing Through Today

One may wonder why a book based on the story of one miracle in the Scriptures would end up serving as an apologetic for Spirit baptism. You might feel that linking the promise of the Spirit to this story is forced, or even wrongheaded altogether. I can understand those objections. I disagree, but I understand.

The woman with the issue of blood teaches us exactly what we need to know to approach God in faith for the promise of the Spirit. Like her, we must begin by recognizing our desperate need for Him. The Spirit's power is the missing link in the life of many Christians, perhaps for no other reason than they have not come to grips with the reality of how badly they need it. Like we learned earlier, those who are not sick do not seek the physician. We've accepted an anemic and powerless version of Christianity because we have been told that the era of power is past, and we've swallowed that lie, hook, line, and sinker.

It's time to get desperate for God.

It's time to become determined, like the woman with the issue of blood, that we will worship Jesus unashamed and seek His power, His glory, and His majesty to be revealed in our lives, in our churches, and in our communities. It's time to believe again that God can do what He has promised and that He is simply waiting for us to ask.

A desperate need. A determined heart. A daring faith. These are exactly what we need if we are to lay hold of God's promises today and to find ourselves in the most unlikely and yet the most rewarding place: the place in His presence *where virtue flows.*

PRAYER

Lord Jesus,

You promised that if we ask our heavenly Father for bread, He will not give us a stone. You invite all who are thirsty to come to You, to receive living water. I believe that what You have promised, You are able also to perform, and I ask You now to baptize me with Your Holy Spirit until I am overflowing with Your presence and power. Reveal Yourself in power, and make me to know that You have done the work, as I submit myself to You.

In Jesus' name, amen!

QUESTIONS FOR REFLECTION
OR SMALL GROUP STUDY

1. How has the promise of power with the baptism of the Spirit been neglected in the modern church? Does God do today what He did in the book of Acts? Why or why not?

2. How has "decision evangelism" sold short the experience of conversion? How can we return to a more biblical and robust experience?

3 Do you agree or disagree with the author's assertion that the Spirit's power is the missing link in the life of many Christians? Explain your answer.

4. Some will disagree with the position taken here about tongues, but it is important not to miss the larger point. In the Scriptures, Spirit baptism is a *conscious experience* with accompanying supernatural signs. If not tongues, what should we expect today?

5. Read Luke 11:13 and Acts 2:39. James writes, "You have not because you ask not" (James 4:2). Have you asked God for the gift of the Holy Spirit?

6. Is it possible for *expectation without agenda* to become an agenda of no expectation? How can we nurture a healthy spiritual longing in our churches so that we truly expect God to show up in a big way?

7. How can the story of the woman with the issue of blood inspire our faith when it comes to seeking God's promises today?

A FINAL WORD

It is madness to wear ladies' straw hats and velvet hats to church; we should all be wearing crash helmets. -Annie Dillard

There are many things we can learn from the woman with the issue of blood, and this little book has been an attempt to draw out some of the more dominant lessons, especially as they relate to our lives today. But make no mistake about it, this story is not an allegory; it is a real story, about a real woman, who had a real need, who met a real Jesus. Her story is important to us today not just because of what it tells us about the ministry of Jesus in the first century, but because of what it continues to tell us about how we approach our Lord today.

Of course, not everything in the narrative finds a perfect parallel to our own situations. For one thing, we are not going to *sneak up* on Jesus. Granted, we cannot be certain whether Jesus really didn't know what had happened, but it doesn't matter either way. We accept the theological proposition that Jesus, as a man, limited Himself to fully embrace our humanity (Philippians 2:6–8). But seated now at the right hand of the throne of God and dwelling in us by the power and presence of the Holy Spirit, Jesus certainly knows our needs, and our hearts, better that we know ourselves. We can approach the throne of grace with confidence because our high priest, Jesus Himself, empathizes with our weaknesses (Hebrews 4:14–16).

One of the things that does seem clear is that being in the presence of Jesus is not the same thing as being changed by His power. While there will always be those who are satisfied to be just another face in the crowd, there will likewise be those who press through. Some will go to church and *blend in*, while others will *enter in* behind the veil. Some will congratulate themselves for their own righteousness, while others will cast all their confidence in God's righteousness. Only the latter sort go home justified. Some will assemble only to pay homage to their doctrinal distinctives, while others will gather to adore the living Lord. The first sort will be smug and satisfied, but will likely leave unchanged, untouched, and unmoved. The second sort will find that they have been transformed by the Master.

What sort will you be?

A lot of what we experience at church, and in our walk with God in general, can be determined by our expectations. Please do not misunderstand me; I am not talking about the power of positive confession or other name-it-and-claim-it nonsense that passes for Christian thinking today. No, I am talking about the way that our understanding of God's Word shapes the way that we approach Him. I am talking about a faith that recognizes that God still rewards those who diligently seek Him. I am speaking of the way that God still keeps His promises, and that when we approach Him on the basis of those promises, we can expect God to be faithful. If we ask Him for bread, He will not give us a stone. He still gives the Holy Spirit to those *who ask* (Luke 11:13). The sad reality is that many Christians have stopped asking.

In this closing chapter, I simply want to encourage you to receive all that God has prepared for you in

Christ Jesus. I want to admonish you to earnestly seek the presence and power of God to invade your church services, your homes, your hearts, and your communities. I want to inspire in you a renewed hunger and thirst for God that will not be satisfied with church as usual.

Allow me to return to the quote at the beginning of this chapter. Only this time, I want to include a little more of the context, so that we can really allow it to stir our hearts. Annie Dillard writes:

> On the whole, I do not find Christians, outside the catacombs, sufficiently sensible of the conditions. Does anyone have the foggiest idea what sort of power we so blithely invoke? Or, as I suspect, does no one believe a word of it? The churches are children playing on the floor with their chemistry sets, mixing up a batch of TNT to kill a Sunday morning. It is madness to wear ladies' straw hats and velvet hats to church; we should all be wearing crash helmets. Ushers should issue life preservers and signal flares; they should lash us to our

pews. For the sleeping god may wake some day and take offense, or the waking god may draw us out to where we can never return.[24]

I don't know the theology of Annie Dillard, but this resonates deeply with me. Contemporary Christian songs like "Oceans" by Hillsong and "Way Beyond Me" by TobyMac speak to the reality of God's desire to do more in us and through us than we could do by our own power, abilities, or wisdom. But our church services have become so safe and seeker friendly that an actual move of the Spirit is likely to be shut down and shut out. What we have forgotten is what seekers are truly seeking. It's not smoke machines and light shows. It's not skinny jeans and Hebrew tattoos.

It's Jesus.

They're seeking Jesus.

Let's give them Jesus!

Without Jesus, our relevance becomes irrelevant.

We are handing out free coffee and informational pamphlets, when we should be stringing out caution tape instead. We should be filling our prayer rooms (remember those?) and crying out to God for a visitation of the glory of God that shakes us to our core, that sets captives free, and that awakens God's people to the spiritual heritage we all possess as His children.

Instead, we choose to live beneath our privilege. Writing over fifty years ago, C. S. Lewis chided:

> It would seem that our Lord finds our desires not too strong, but too weak. We are half-hearted creatures, fooling about with drink and sex and ambition when infinite joy is offered us, like an ignorant child who wants to go on making mud pies in a slum because he cannot imagine what is meant by the offer of a holiday at the sea. We are far too easily pleased.[25]

If there is anything that I pray this book has done for you, it is to stir up your desire for more of God. To make you refuse to settle for religious posturing instead of revival fire. To inspire you to press through when others won't. There are far too many places in the world today where God is doing the miraculous for us to wag our heads and continue to speak of the cessation of the gifts.

In America, we have not because we ask not. We

ask not because we believe not. But the Spirit is moving around the world where people are hurting, hungry, and unhindered by the "safe" spirituality of the West. He will do it here, but only when we recognize our desperate need, only when we become determined to touch Him regardless of the cost, and only when we believe with daring faith that God will meet us in power.

His virtue still flows. *Press through and lay hold!*

NOTES

1. Matthew 15:21–28; Luke 19:1–10; Mark 10:46–52; Matthew 8:1–4, and Mark 5:25–34, respectively.

2. Mark 5:25–34, New King James Version. See also Matthew 9:20–22, and Luke 8:43–48.

3. Dr. Lightfoot cites many examples from Bab. Shabb. fol. 110.

4. For those who might like to boast in their spiritual pedigree, consider how Paul felt about his in Philippians 3:3–9.

5. *I Need Thee Every Hour*, hymn by Annie S. Hawks, 1835–1918; music by Robert Lowry, 1826–1899.

6. A. W. Tozer, *Whatever Happened to Worship?: A Call to True Worship* (Camp Hills: WingSpread Publishers, 2006).

7. A. W. Tozer, *The Dangers of a Shallow Faith: Awakening from Spiritual Lethargy* (Bloomington: Bethany House Publishers, 2012).

8. The Tosefta records a tradition that "upon the death of the last prophets, Haggai, Zechariah, and Malachi, the Holy Spirit departed from Israel" (Sota 13:3).

9. Quoted from a sermon and shared by R. T. Kendall in *Holy Fire: A Balanced, Biblical Look at the Holy Spirit's Work in Our Lives* (Lake Mary: Charisma House, 2014).

10. John 4:46–54.

11. This paragraph adapted from *Dirty God: Jesus with the Lepers* by Johnnie Moore. Published July 1, 2013, on faithgateway.com.

12. I can't help but think of the man at the pool of Bethesda who was healed by Jesus (John 5) and later found in the Temple (v. 14), a place that had been previously off-limits because of his condition.

13. There is a wonderful illustration of this in Ezekiel 16:8, where God speaks of entering into covenant with Israel, saying, "I spread the corner of my garment over you and covered your naked body. I gave you my solemn oath and entered into a covenant with you, declares the Sovereign LORD, and you became mine" (see also Psalm 91:4).

14. Ann Spangler and Lois Tverberg, *Sitting at the Feet of Rabbi Jesus* (Grand Rapids: Zondervan, 2009), 150.

15. J. D. Greear *Jesus, Continued ...: Why the Spirit Inside You Is Better than Jesus Beside You* (Grand Rapids: Zondervan, 2014).

16. I wish I knew where this quote originates. I have seen it all over the Internet and read it in Greear's book (above), as well as in R. T. Kendall's *Holy Fire: A Balanced, Biblical Look at the Holy Spirit's Work in Our Lives.*

17. R. T. Kendall, *Holy Fire: A Balanced, Biblical Look at the Holy Spirit's Work in Our Lives.*

18. A. W. Tozer, *The Pursuit of God* (North Charlestown: CreateSpace, 2016).

19. Steve Bremner, *Nine Lies People Believe About Speaking in Tongues* (Shippensburg: Destiny Image Publishers, 2016) 147.

20. John R. W. Stott, *The Message of Acts* (Downers Grove: InterVarsity Press, 1990) 67.

21. M. Eugene Boring and Fred B. Craddock, *The People's New Testament Commentary* (Louisville: Westminster John Knox Press, 2010). To be fair, the commentators are not making a case for tongues. They add, "You cannot tell whence the Spirit comes or whither it goes, but you can hear its voice when it does come. So, by hearing the voice of the Spirit, is every one born of the Spirit. He who receives by faith the communications of the Spirit is born of the Spirit." I use the quote only to illustrate the connection between wind and Spirit (the same word in Greek), and between the "sound of the wind" and the "voice of the Spirit," which is a fair rendering of the text. Theologians come to various conclusions on how to understand or interpret "the voice of the Spirit." Applying a Pentecostal hermeneutic to the text provides a valuable and valid perspective, but it should be noted that there is much room here for disagreement and debate.

22. See the entire C&MA position on spiritual gifts at https:// www.cmalliance.org/about/beliefs/perspectives/ spiritual-gifts.

23. A. B. Simpson, May 1908, C&MA Annual Report; see also A. B. Simpson, "Spiritual Sanctity," as recorded in Richard Gilbertson, *The Baptism of the Holy Spirit: The Views of A. B. Simpson and His Contemporaries* (Camp Hill: Christian Publications, 1993), 322, where Simpson writes, "Our warning is against the danger of exaggerating [tongues], of seeking it for its own sake rather than seeking the Spirit Himself, and of exercising it in an extravagant and unscriptural way to the dishonor of Christ, the disorder of His work and the division of His people." No arguments there. The problem is when our determination to *expect with no agenda* leads to *an agenda of no expectation*. That is sadly where many churches have ended up.

24. Annie Dillard, *Teaching a Stone to Talk* (New York: HarperCollins, 2009).

25. C. S. Lewis, *The Weight of Glory* (Grand Rapids: Zondervan, 2001).

ACKNOWLEDGEMENTS

There have been many people over the years who have told me, "There's a book inside you!" I felt it myself, but allowed self-doubt and perfectionism to paralyze me to the point of inaction. I am still my own worst critic. A college education definitely helped, as the constant demands of academia forced me to write even when I didn't feel like it. Nothing is quite as inspiring as last-minute panic.

With that in mind, I feel I owe the largest debt of gratitude to my good friend Mike Ritter, who refused to let me talk about the book I was *going to write* one day, and gave me specific deadlines to meet for each chapter until the final draft was complete. Excuses wouldn't work. Forget the fact that I was also pastoring a church, teaching as an adjunct professor, and at the same time taking classes to finish my Master of Divinity. No, if the chapter was due, it was due.

So here we are.

While there are many others I might thank for their influence and encouragement, I simply want to recognize my good friend Mike. *You are a great friend.*

ABOUT THE AUTHOR

Mark Kennicott, with his wife, Zulmita, and four children (Zachary, Joshua, Elena, and Elisa), have lived in Minnesota since 2008, after leaving Central Florida to follow God's call to the Midwest. He has served in various ministry capacities, most recently as lead pastor for Living Water Christian Church, an Assembly of God congregation in Shakopee, Minnesota.

Mark earned his undergraduate degree, as well as two master's degrees (a Master of Arts in Christian Studies and a Master of Divinity) from Crown College (crown.edu), where he now serves as an adjunct professor, teaching both Old and New Testament history in their online undergraduate program.

When he is not engaged in ministry, writing, or teaching, Mark enjoys spending time with his family, rock climbing, and disc golf.

Where Virtue Flows is his first book.

The author can be reached at kennicottm@gmail.com

Printed in the United States
By Bookmasters